The Way of the Donkey

Nancy Willard

The Way of the Donkey

Nancy Willard

Embrace Civility in the Digital Age

© 2019 Nancy Willard. All Rights Reserved. No part of this book may be reproduced or utilized in any form or by any means, electronic or mechanical, including photocopying, recording, or by any information storage and retrieval system, without written permission from the author.

Willard, Nancy

The Way of the Donkey

ISBN 978-0-9724236-5-6

Library of Congress Control Number

1. Donkeys. 2. Positive Psychology. 3. Trauma Informed.

Embrace Civility in the Digital Age

Website: http://embracecivility.org

The Way of the Donkey

Website: http://donkeyeeaw.org

Table of Contents

Let's Learn About Donkeys ~ 1

Donkeys Serving People Through Time ~ 11

Amazing Things Donkeys Are Doing Now ~ 25

Spiritual Donkeys ~ 41

Following The Way of the Donkey ~ 51

On the front and back cover are the author's donkeys who are in training to provide donkey therapy. Income from the sales of this book will go to establish a sanctuary where these donkeys (and hopefully more) can bring joy to many.

On the back cover are Dominique, Opie, June Bug, Bella, Sweet Pea, and Orion. (Orion is a rescue and does not like hats.) Dante, the author's BLM burro is on the front cover and this page.

Educators and parents can find more information about the positive psychology and trauma informed research basis of the insight that is set forth in on the author's web site at http://donkeyeeaw.org.

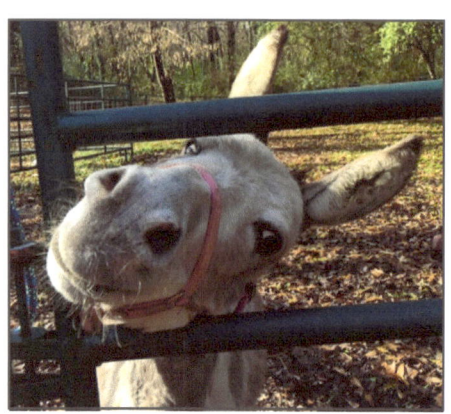

Let's Learn About Donkeys!

Let's learn about donkeys!

Do you want to learn all about donkeys? Donkeys are really cool animals. Donkeys love people—babies, kids, teens, adults, and older people.

The best things about donkeys are their loving eyes and warm soft ears.

When donkeys use their voice it sounds like they are saying "EEAW." This is called "braying." Donkeys have very loud voices. You can hear a donkey braying for about 2 miles or 3 kilometers. When a donkey says "EEAW" everyone smiles. Sometimes it looks like donkeys are also smiling or laughing.

A male donkey is called "jack." A female donkey is called "jenny." The Spanish name for a donkey is "burro." Donkeys can live for a very long time—up to 40 years.

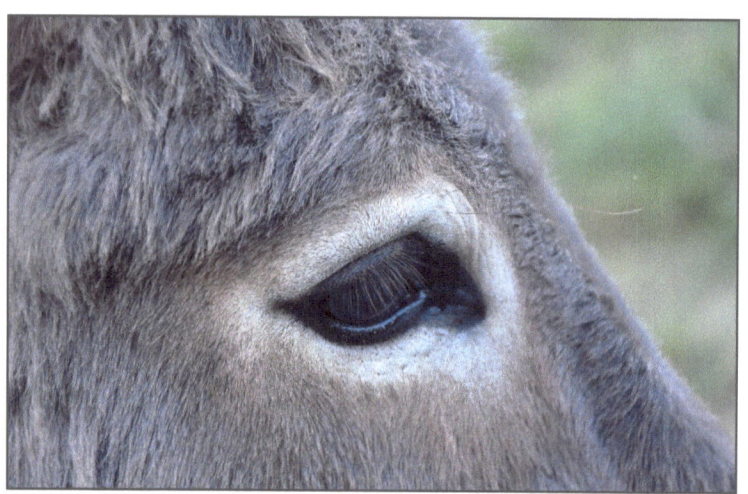

Donkeys in Different Sizes!

People are measured by feet and inches or centimeters. Equines are measured by "hands." Before measuring tapes, people would figure out how tall an equine was by using their hands. They would place one hand on top of the other from the ground up to the equine's "withers." Withers are the equine's shoulders. A "hand" is 4 inches or 10 centimeters—about the size of an adult hand.

Donkeys come in three different sizes: small, medium, and large.

- **Small.** Miniature donkeys. They are about 9 hands. This is around three feet or 91 centimeters tall. They weigh 200 to 400 pounds or 90 to 180 kilograms. A child weighing up to 50 pounds or 23 kilograms can ride a miniature donkey. Miniature donkeys are primarily used as pets.

- **Medium.** Standard donkeys. Most are about 12 hands. This is around 4 feet or 122 centimeters tall. They weigh 400 to 750 pounds or 180 to 340 kilograms. A child or teen weighing up to 100 pounds or 45 kilograms can ride a standard donkey. Some standards are smaller. There are also larger standards that can carry more weight. Most standard donkeys in the world are working donkeys.

- **Large.** Mammoth donkeys. They are 13.2 to over 14 hands. This is over 5 feet or 152 centimeters tall. They can weigh 1,000 to 2,000 pounds or 450 to 900 kilograms. A child, teen, or adult can ride a mammoth donkey. Mammoth donkeys are used to breed with horses to create mules.

Donkey Colors and Hooves

Most donkeys are gray. However, donkeys can also be black, red, brown, white, frosty, and spotted. Almost all donkeys have a stripe down their back and over their shoulders. This forms a cross or "t."

In regions where it is cold, donkeys have very thick fur during winter. They shed this fur in spring. Most donkeys are naturally sleek during the summer. Some donkeys, like the Poitou donkey from France is very shaggy all of the time.

They love to be "groomed." Groomed means brushing.

Donkey's hooves are always growing, just like your finger nails. Their hooves have to be trimmed by a "farrier." A farrier is a person who trims the feet of donkey, horses, and mules. Just like it does not hurt to trim your finger nails, it does not hurt the donkey to have its hooves trimmed.

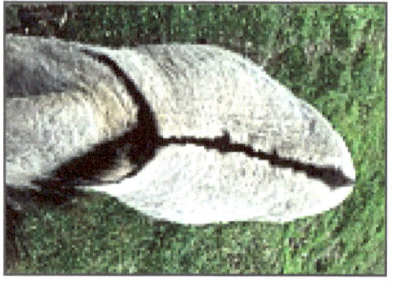

Evolution of Equines

It took over 50 million years for equines to "evolve" on our planet. Evolve means to develop and change slowly over time. Animals evolved because of how our planet developed and changed slowly over time.

The first equine was called the Eohippus. This was a small animal about the size of a fox. Over millions of years, different kinds of equines evolved and spread throughout the world. They got lots bigger. Scientists gave them very funny names like Orohippus, Epihippus, Mesohippus, Miohippus, Kalobatippus, Parahippus, Merychippus, Hipparion, Pliohippus, Dinohippus, Plesippus, and lastly, Equus. Try to say this fast!

The last common ancestor of horses, zebras, and donkeys was Equus. Equus lived 4 to 4.5 million years ago. From this time on, there were only three kinds of equines. The scientific name for a horse is "equus caballus," for a zebra is "equus quagga," and for a donkey is "equus asinus."

Equines are considered "one-toed ungulates." Ungulate means they have a hoof. One toe means their hoof is just one piece. Cows, sheep, goats, and deer are "two-toed ungulates."

THE WILD AFRICAN ASS

Donkeys evolved in Africa. The wild donkey is called a Wild African Ass. It is considered okay to use the word "ass" when describing a donkey. But it is not considered polite to use this word in other ways. There were two kinds of Wild African Asses, the Nubian Wild Ass and the Somali Wild Ass. It is presumed that the Nubian Wild Ass is "extinct." Extinct means there are no more of these animals.

There are still Somali Wild African Asses in Africa. Unfortunately, they are considered "endangered." Endangered means they may not be around for much longer. Their "habitat" is being destroyed. Habitat means the natural home or environment where an animal lives.

Donkeys Stop and Think Things Through

Donkeys behave differently from horses because of what the environment was like where they evolved.

Horses evolved on wide open plains. If horses sense danger, they just start running. They do not take the time to look more closely. They just assume that the rustle in the bush is something that is going to try to eat them. So away they run–without looking back.

Donkeys evolved in places that were more hilly and rocky. If they just ran, they would risk tripping and falling. That would not be very smart. And donkeys are very smart.

When donkeys sense that something might be dangerous, they will stop. They will stand very tall to make themselves look as powerful as possible–so that whatever might want to eat them will think again. They will take the time to think things through before deciding what to do. A donkey may decide to run from danger, but will pick out the path carefully. A donkey may decide to fight by kicking. Or a donkey may decide it really was not something dangerous after all and go back to eating.

Even when lions are not a risk, donkeys still stop, stand tall, and think things through if they think that something might be dangerous, feel unsure, or are not happy. Some people consider them to be stubborn. What they are doing is being careful to protect themselves.

MULES AND ZONKEYS

Donkeys can be "bred" with horses or zebras. Bred means when a male and female equine have a baby.

A horse that is bred by a donkey will have a baby that is called a "mule." Mules are excellent work animals. They are stronger and more sure-footed than either horses or donkeys.

A donkey bred by a zebra will have a baby called a "zonkey." Zonkeys are often wild like the zebra. So they are not very useful. They are really cute.

Donkey Babies

One of the most wonderful things about donkeys is donkey babies. Mother donkeys take very good care of their babies. Donkey babies love to take a quick drink of milk from their mom. Donkey babies love to run. They love to roll in the dirt. They love to have fun with other donkey babies. Then after lots of time spent exploring the world, they just need to lie down for a nap.

Donkey Babies and Kids

There is nothing more fun than hanging out with donkey babies! Which one do you think is the baby mammoth donkey baby?

Donkeys Serving People Through Time

Donkeys in Egypt

Donkeys were first "domesticated" in Egypt around 5000 BCE. Domesticated means tamed and used by people. Egypt is a country in the Middle East. Egypt is famous for its pyramids.

Donkeys were the first kind of animal ever to be used to carry things for people or to be ridden. Sometimes, this is called being a "beast of burden." Pictures of donkeys were drawn on the walls of the pyramids showing how they were used for carrying harvest.

The pyramids were built to be graves for the "pharaohs." Pharaohs were the rulers in ancient Egypt. In one early pharaoh's grave, ten donkeys were buried in a ceremonial way. From a study of the bones of the donkeys, scientists could tell that the donkeys had been used in service. The fact that donkeys were buried in this way shows how valued donkeys were in this society.

Donkeys for Farming, Transport, and Trade

Donkeys were used for carrying things on their backs. They were able to carry things like firewood, bricks, or wheat. Donkeys also could be ridden or pull a cart. Donkeys were also used in mills to pull a mill stone around to grind grain into flour.

Because they were able to carry things, donkeys were used for "trade." Trade means selling things, called "goods," to someone or buying goods from someone. Donkeys were able to carry goods that traders wanted to sell to those who lived in other villages. They could also carry the blankets and food for the traders who were traveling from place to place to sell their goods. Sometimes they also carried traders.

Because donkeys were able to be used for trade, this helped people living in different places in the world sell goods to each other and get to know each other.

In addition to the goods they were carrying, the donkeys were also sold to the people who lived in other parts of the world. Their new owners would then use them for carrying things and people, farming, and trade in these new places. Donkeys became spread throughout the world through the trading routes.

DONKEYS AND THE ROMAN EMPIRE

The Roman Empire lasted from around 27 BCE to 476 CE. The Romans came from Rome, Italy, which is in Southern Europe. The Romans were in power in many parts of the Middle East and Europe throughout this time.

The Romans took donkeys with them to carry supplies when they went to "conquer" other people. Conquer means to take control of people using military force. The Romans brought donkeys from Southern Europe into Northern Europe when they travelled to conquer these places. Donkeys were brought to the British Isles when the Romans conquered the people there in 43 CE.

In the areas the Romans conquered, donkeys were then used for farming, transport, and trade. The Romans also used the donkeys to work in vineyards, where the grapes were grown for wine.

Donkeys on the Silk Road

Donkeys were used for trade along the Silk Road. The Silk Road was a network of trade routes connecting China and the Far East with the Middle East and Europe. The Silk Road was established when the Han Dynasty in China officially opened trade with the West in 130 BCE. The Silk Road routes remained in use until 1453 CE.

Donkeys came all the way from the Middle East to China even before the Silk Road was established. Scientists have discovered that the donkeys in China originated from the Nubian Wild Ass and the Somali Wild Ass. Significantly more donkeys came to China when the Silk Road trading increased.

The Silk Road was about 7,000 miles or 11,300 kilometers long. Traders on the Silk Road did not travel the entire Silk Road. The trader would travel part of of the Silk Road to trade with another trader and then return home. Then that trader would take the goods to another trading post. This way goods would be carried the entire Silk Road, from China to France and back–and all places in between.

This is how silk, spices, paper, and gun powder from China ended up in France and wool, silver, and gold ended up in China. The Silk Road was also responsible for the expansion of language, culture, religious beliefs, philosophy and science.

The Silk Road was very important in introducing people who were living in different parts of the world to each other. Donkeys played an important role in bringing people together.

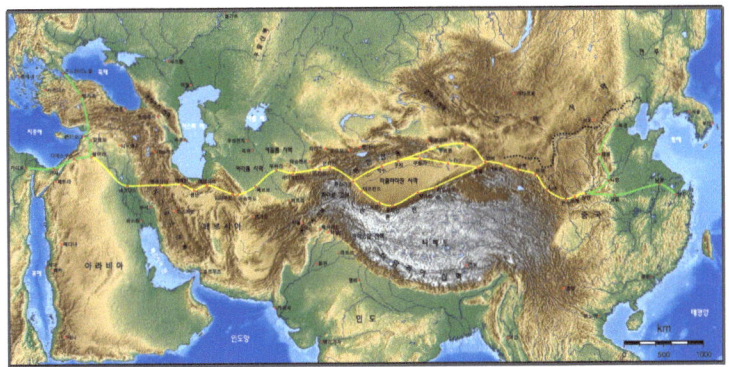

Donkeys Come to the New World

Donkeys, horses, and mules were very useful in Spain, which is in Southern Europe. Christopher Columbus was from Italy. In 1492 CE, Christopher Columbus led an exploration, funded by Spain, to try to find a new route to China for trade. He ended up finding the New World, which is North, Central, and South America.

On his second voyage to the New World in 1495 CE, Columbus brought donkeys, horses, and mules. More donkeys, horses, and mules were brought from Spain on additional trips across the ocean by the Spaniards. This was called the Spanish Conquest.

When Columbus came to the New World he was acting under what is now referred to as the Doctrine of Discovery. In the 1400's, the Pope, who was the head of the Catholic Church, gave the Catholic countries in Europe the right to conquer and exploit the native people and their lands in the New World.

The people in European countries thought they were superior to those living in the New World. The bottom pictures show the evidence of the great civilizations that were present in the New World before the Europeans came. The Pyramid of the Sun in Teotihuacan was built about 200 CE and the Aztecs Pyramid at St. Cecilia Acatitlan was built starting in 1325 CE. Both of these are in what is now Mexico. In addition, Machu Picchu, which was built starting around 1450 CE, is in what is now Peru.

Unfortunately, donkeys were used as part of this exploitation of native people in the New World. However, donkeys have been used by people in these lands for farming, transport, and trade ever since.

Mules in Europe and the United States

The exact origin of mules is not clear. It appears that mules were bred in the Middle East since around 3000 BCE. Mules were considered to be more valuable than either horses or donkeys even in this time. In Medieval Europe horses were bred to be large to carry armored knights. Mules were a preferred riding animal. They were also used in agriculture, primarily for plowing.

The first president of the United States, George Washington, is sometimes called "The Father of the Country." He could also be called "The Father of the American Mule." Washington was very active in promoting the use of mules for farming to build agricultural business in the new United States.

In 1785 CE, the King of Spain found out that Washington wanted some mammoth donkeys. The King sent two mammoth donkeys to Washington on a ship. Unfortunately, one died. The other donkey was named Royal Gift. An advertisement for breeding services of Royal Gift is in the museum at Mount Vernon, which was Washington's home.

Mules became very popular for farming until the invention of the engine, which led to the invention of tractors that could pull plows. To create mules requires that some people own mammoth donkey jacks.

Donkeys Help Search for Gold

Standard donkeys were used by prospectors who were searching for gold and silver in the western United States in the 19th century. The donkeys that the prospectors used came from the donkeys that were brought to this region by the Spanish. Because the Spanish name for donkey is "burro," the standard donkeys that were used by the prospectors were called burros.

Burros carried the prospector's belongings and mining equipment. This included the prospector's blankets and food, as well as their pick axes and mining pans. With all of this mining gear hooked onto a pack saddle on their back, it was not possible for the prospector to also ride their burro.

When the gold rush ended, these burros were released into the wild. They are now called "wild burros." They are actually "feral" donkeys. Feral means that they were once domesticated, but were released and have been running wild. They are not wild like the Wild African Ass. Burros are still running wild in the Southwest of the United States.

Smart Donkeys in Australia

Donkeys were brought to Australia in the 1860's to be used as pack animals. Before this, horses had been used as pack animals. There was a plant in Australia that was poisonous for horses. It was said the plant was not poisonous for donkeys. Perhaps donkeys were smart enough not to eat this plant.

Some of these donkeys were released into the wild. There are now many feral donkeys in Australia. These donkeys live in the same areas where kangaroos and koalas live. Do you think they might be friends?

The donkeys in these pictures were wild. They are now being cared for by A Donkeys Trust.

There are seven continents in the world. These are Africa, Antarctica, Asia, Australia, Europe, North America, and South America. With the coming of donkeys to Australia, there were donkeys on six of the seven continents. There are no donkeys in Antartica. It is too cold. No donkey friends for penguins.

Miniature Donkeys from the Mediterranean to the U.S.

Miniature donkeys were bred and used in the Mediterranean islands of Sicily and Sardinia. The people in these islands created brightly colored carts to be pulled by the donkeys. These carts are still used on these islands today.

Several miniature donkeys were brought from Sicily and Sardinia to the United States starting in 1929. These donkeys were called "Mediterranean donkeys." The people who bought these donkeys were all quite wealthy. They purchased these donkeys for pets.

Some of the people who owned these donkeys began to carefully breed them. The American Donkey & Mule Association and the National Miniature Donkey Association began registering these donkeys and promoting them. These breeders made sure that the miniature donkeys were healthy and sound. Below is a National Champion Miniature Donkey.

Because of the work of these breeders, miniature donkeys have become very popular in the United States as family pets and for showing. Many people now are able to own these donkeys. Miniature donkeys can also now be found in other countries.

Donkeys in Battle

During World War I, standard donkeys were used to support the troops who were fighting in Europe. They carried packs of artillery shells, equipment, and food and water to the front line. They rescued wounded soldiers from the battlefields. They even had their own gas masks. During World War II, donkeys and mules were used in the same way but there were more tanks and trucks then.

Donkeys became very popular among troops. One problem was that the donkeys tended to bray–EEAW! This created a risk that they might reveal troop positions to the enemy.

Donkeys in Aesop's Fables

Aesop was a storyteller believed to have lived in ancient Greece between 620 and 564 BCE. There are many stories it is said he told, which are called Aesop's Fables. His fables were spoken. Since his time, these fables have been rewritten many times by many different people. All of the fables have an important message. In these stories, donkeys are called "asses."

A book with pictures called *Baby's Own Aesop* was created by Walter Crane in 1887. These are some of the stories and illustrations of asses from this book.

Town Musicians of Bremen

Jakob and Wilhelm Grimm, published fairy tales from 1812 to 1857. These are called Grimm's Fairy Tales. One of their famous tales featured a donkey who was friends with other animals.

A donkey, a dog, a cat, and a rooster were all very old and no longer useful on their farms. They left their homes and set out together. They decide to go to the town of Bremen to live without owners. They planned to become musicians.

On their way, they saw a lighted cottage. When they looked inside they saw four robbers. They stood on each other's backs and scared the robbers away by making very loud noises. The animal musicians then ate a good meal and went to sleep.

Later that night, the robbers returned. One robber investigated. He saw the cat's eyes and thought this was the fire. The cat scratched his face, the dog bit him on the leg, the donkey kicked him, and the rooster crowed. He ran out the door, screaming. He told the other robbers that he was scratched by a witch, cut with a knife, hit with a club, and screamed at by a judge.

The robbers abandoned the cottage. The animal musicians lived there happily for the rest of their days.

DONKEYS AT WORK

The photographs on this page are all from the late 1800's and early 1900's. The first automobile was invented at this time, but they were not available for many people. Donkeys were working around the world doing the same jobs they had done from when the Egyptians first started using them in 5000 BCE.

Amazing Things Donkeys are Doing Now

Donkeys Are Still At Work

At this time, there are around 40 million donkeys in the world. With the invention of the automobile, along with trucks and farming equipment, the use of donkeys as working animals in industrialized countries has vanished. However, in the poorest parts of Asia, Africa, Central America, and South America, donkeys continued to be vitally important in working and providing service to families.

These donkeys are the standard size donkey. Donkeys still carrying things and people and they still pull carts. They still support farming, transport, and trade. No other animal in the world has provided such valuable services to people for this long.

Donkeys for Family Fun

In the 1960's, donkeys started to became popular for people to own as pets. Families with children especially like to have donkeys.

Donkeys are used for riding, leading, and pulling carts—or just hanging around for fun. Donkeys are great for children to ride. They are smaller than horses. They are more friendly than ponies. They also do not run away if something strange or scary happens. Riding a donkey is very safe.

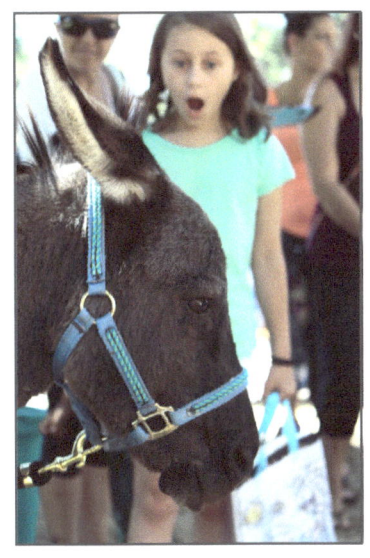

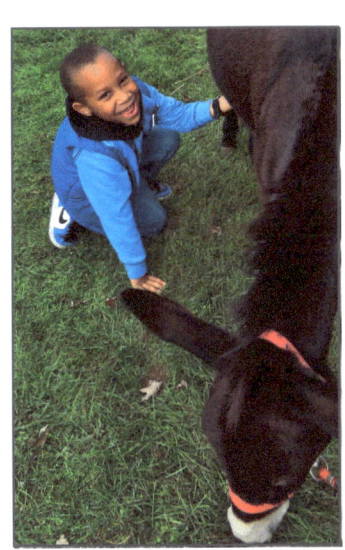

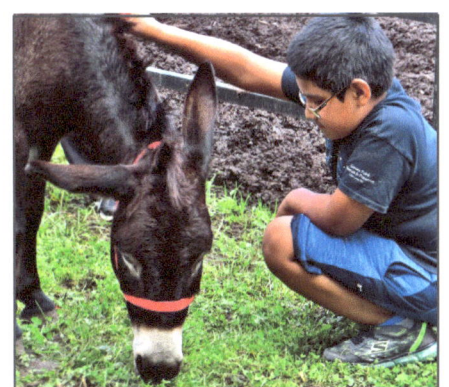

Donkey Shows

Some donkey owners like to take their donkeys to compete with other donkeys in donkey shows.

At these shows, donkeys can compete in "conformation classes." Conformation classes are where donkeys are judged how they look. There are also classes for in-hand showing, where the donkeys are led in the ring. Some of the classes involve riding. Donkeys also compete by driving carts, jumping, or going through obstacle courses. Sometimes, there are even donkey costume classes. One fun kind of a show is a mountain trail competition, where horses, mules, and donkeys all compete on a course that looks like a mountain trail. Donkeys are really good at doing mountain trails.

Adults and children can compete in donkey shows. Some shows are for all sizes of donkeys. Some are for all equines. There are also shows for just one size of donkey, like shows for miniature donkeys.

WILD BURROS IN SOUTHWEST UNITED STATES

In the Southwest United States there are herds of wild burros. They are actually feral, not wild. They came from the burros that were let go by the prospectors. These were burros brought to the region from Spain They are the standard size burros that have been used for service since the Egyptians.

Many of these wild burros are on lands managed by the United States government by the Bureau of Land Management or BLM. Feral horses, called wild horses, also are on these lands. Sometimes, the BLM gathers wild burros because there are too many of them running on the land. They sell these burros to people who want to tame them. At first, the burros are afraid, but it is possible to tame and train them.

You can tell if a wild burro came from the BLM because it will have a white brand on its neck. It did not hurt the burro to have this brand put on. The brand tells where and when they were captured.

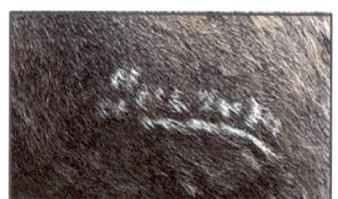

Pack Burro Racing

A sport called pack burro racing is incredibly exciting and fun–if you and your donkey are in really good shape and like to run. Pack Burro Racing started in Colorado. This fun sport has spread to other states.

The idea for Pack Burro Racing grew out of use of burros by 19th century prospectors. If a prospector discovered gold or silver in the mountains, he would have to race back to the nearest town to be the first person to stake a claim. Because their burros were carrying all of their equipment, the prospectors could not ride them. If two prospectors discovered gold or silver at the same place, they would have to race each other back to town. The first prospector to get to the claim office got the claim. Hence, a race.

The Western Pack Burro Ass-ociation has sponsored Pack Burro Racing in Colorado every summer since 1949. These races can be up to 30 miles or 48 kilometers long. All sizes of burros compete. The racers lead their burros over mountain trails and roads. Every burro must have a pack saddle with pick, shovel, and gold pan–just like when they were assisting prospectors.

Donkey Trail Riding

Donkeys can be used for trail riding or backpacking in mountain wilderness areas. People may ride their donkeys, ride horses and lead their donkeys, or just walk and lead their donkeys. If they are not being ridden, the donkeys have a pack saddle to carry tents, sleeping bags, and food.

Donkey Trekking

Donkey trekking is popular throughout Europe, especially Southern Europe. Donkeys carry pack saddles for people who want to enjoy walking with donkeys through the countryside. Children can also ride the donkeys. Going for a walk or ride in the beautiful countryside and exploring old villages with a long ear friend is lots of fun.

Donkey trekking can be day trips or even longer. For the longer trips, the people walk along a trail with their donkey for the day. Then, at night, there are places where they can eat a good meal and go to sleep in a bed. The donkeys are also cared for at these stops. Everyone wakes up the next morning, has breakfast or some hay, and they are off on the trail for a great time.

Mules at Work and Having Fun

Mules are still used in some regions of the world in agriculture, just as they have been used for centuries. Mules are also popular for riding, just like horses.

Mules are used by the United States Forest Service to help maintain trails and to fight forest fires in the mountains. Mules carry food, water, and other supplies to the firefighters. They can go up into the mountains where cars and helicopters cannot go. Because mules are half donkey, they remain very calm and do not go into flight if they have to go through smoky areas or through other dangers.

In the Grand Canyon, mules are used to take people down to the river and back. The Grand Canyon is in Arizona in the United States.

It is necessary that some people own mammoth jack donkeys to breed with horses to create these mules.

Donkey Weddings and Parties

Adorable donkeys dressed up with flowers and finery provide a great addition to weddings and parties.

Donkeys are great at greeting guests. Donkeys are very good at helping people get to know each other. Donkeys can escort the bride down the aisle—or maybe the groom. They can walk down the aisle with the flower girl or ring bearer. They can be in the photos. They might have a pack saddle and deliver drinks and snacks at a party.

Donkey Therapy

People use donkeys for "donkey therapy." Donkeys make people feel really happy. Sometimes, people will bring donkeys to nursing homes or hospitals to visit people who are sick or older. Donkeys can go to schools. People can come to where the donkeys live to ride a donkey or lead a donkey around the arena. Or they may spend time grooming a donkey. Someone with special needs may own a donkey to be a friend.

Amber was born prematurely. The doctors had to put a tube in her throat so she could breathe. But this made it so that she could not talk. When Shocks the donkey was rescued by the Donkey Sanctuary in the United Kingdom, he was covered in big sores. He was very sad. When Shocks had healed, he started working in The Donkey Sanctuary's donkey therapy program. Amber came and met Shocks. Amber was able to ride Shocks and lead him around the arena. They became good friends. Finally, Amber had surgery that would allow her to talk. But no one knew whether she would be able to talk. Soon after this, when Amber was with Shocks, she said her very first words: "I love you Shocky."

Harrison's parents are pack burro racers. Harrison has autism. Harrison has been riding donkeys since he was very young. He rode a donkey on a camping trip when he was three years old. If he is having a tough time, his parents send him outside to be with the donkeys. This helps Harrison become calm. Being able to handle donkeys has helped Harrison understand that he can be successful in many other ways.

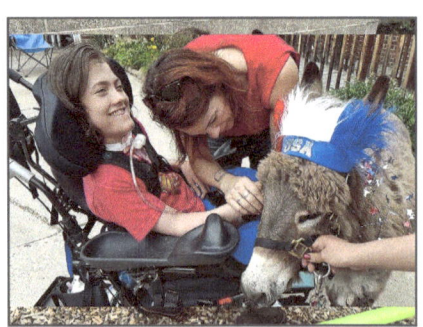

Donkey Rescue

Unfortunately, sometimes donkeys are not treated well. They may be abused or neglected. Sometimes donkeys are sold at auction and may be taken to places where they will not be safe. Organizations have been established in different parts of the world that engage in donkey rescue. The Donkey Sanctuary in the United Kingdom and Peaceful Valley Donkey Rescue in the United States are the two largest rescue organizations. Sometimes, people find out about donkeys that need to be rescued and reach out to bring them to safety and a happy home.

Daisy, the donkey with the little girl below, was rescued from a bad place. The middle picture was taken 15 minutes after she arrived home. She knew she was safe. Daisy still loves hugs. Daisy now works as a therapy donkey with young people. Piper, the baby donkey, was rescued with her mom from a bad place. Now Piper visits hospitals as a therapy donkey. Hazel is a rescue donkey who absolutely loves music.

There may be a donkey rescue located next to you. Donkey rescues are usually non-profit organizations. They depend on donations to help them care for the donkeys. They love to have people come to visit.

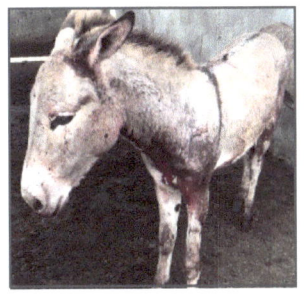

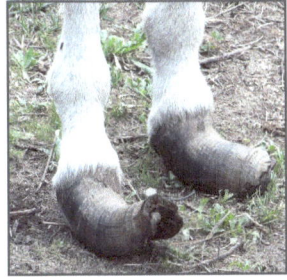

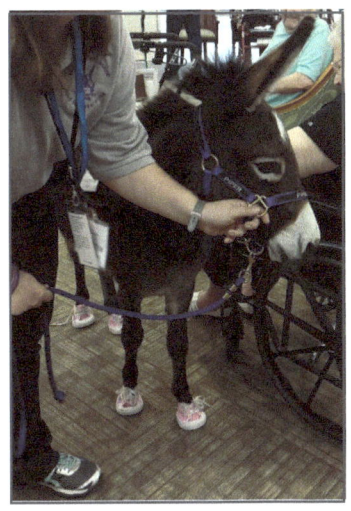

Donkey Basketball

Donkey basketball is a cruel event used for fundraising. Donkey basketball is disrespectful and harmful for donkeys. The event resembles basketball and is played on a basketball court. The human players must sit on the donkeys when they are shooting and passing a basketball.

Most human players do not know how to handle donkeys. Donkeys might stop because they do not like what is happening to them. So to convince a donkey to move, the player can become hurtful. Donkeys might be dragged or pulled. Then everyone laughs at the "stubborn" donkeys.

Another big concern about donkey basketball is the weight of the players. This event uses standard donkeys. Standard donkeys should not carry a person who weighs more than around 100 pounds or 45 kilograms. Often people who are much heavier ride these donkeys. This can hurt these donkeys.

Donkey basketball teaches people that it is okay to treat animals with disrespect and to ignore their safety and how they are feeling. It teaches people that watching someone being cruel to an animal is something to laugh at.

If an event like this comes to your town, you could be an "advocate" against this. An advocate is someone who speaks up and says, "this is not okay" when something is happening that is not right. You could write a letter to the editor of your newspaper that explains what you know about how wonderful donkeys are and why this is hurtful to them. If a school is doing this, you could go and talk to the school board.

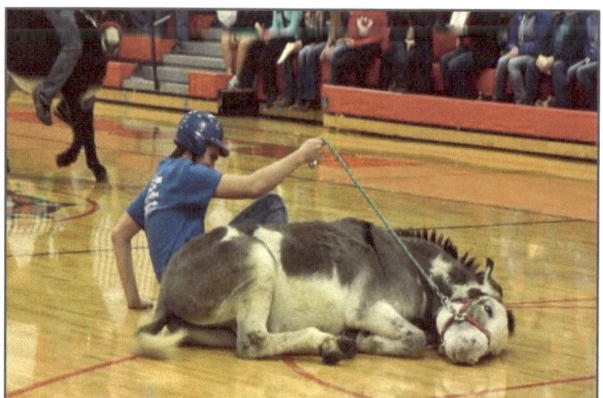

Spiritual Donkeys

GREEK MYTHOLOGY

Dionysus

Dionysus was the god of vineyards, where they grow grapes to make wine. He was known as the god of "merriment." Merriment means a happy time. Dionysus was frequently pictured riding on a donkey.

Hera, who was queen of the gods, did not like Dionysus. She caused him to go mad and wander throughout the world. One time, Dionysus was trying to reach an "oracle" to ask how he could get rid of the madness. An oracle is someone who has great wisdom. As he traveled to find this oracle, he came to a lake that he could not cross. But along came two donkeys. One donkey offered to carry him across the water. The donkey was being of service. Dionysus was so grateful that he put the two donkeys in the sky as two stars. This was considered a high honor in those days.

Hephaestus

Hephaestus was the god of fire, blacksmiths, metal arts, and volcanoes. He was the son of Zeus and Hera. When he was born, he was so ugly that Hera threw him out of Mount Olympus. He fell very far and landed in the sea. He broke his leg and it became deformed. He was brought up by sea nymphs. Hephaestus worked very hard in blacksmithing and metal arts. He made many clever inventions with metal. He even made himself a magical wheeled chair that he could travel in, since he had a disability.

Hephaestus also made presents for Hera, who he was still angry with. One time, he sent her a golden throne. Hera loved it. But when she sat in it, she was magically tied up by numerous invisible cords Hephaestus had created. She was stuck in this throne for days. Hephaestus refused to let her go. His friend Dionysus was the only god he trusted. Dionysus got Hephaestus drunk on wine. He then put him on a donkey and took him to Mount Olympus. Hephaestus finally undid the invisible cords and let Hera go. After this, he was allowed to live on Mount Olympus.

EEAW! Scares the Giants

Zeus, the king of the gods, had declared war on the giants. He called all of the gods to the fight. Some gods came riding on donkeys. When they got close to the fighting the donkeys became so afraid they started braying. The giants had never heard such a sound. They became frightened and quickly ran away.

Hinduism

Shitala Mata is a goddess who is worshiped by Hindus. The Hindu religion started in India, which is in Asia. The Hindu gods and goddesses have animals or birds that they travel on and who support their work. They are called "vahanas." The vahanas of Shitala Mata is a donkey.

Shitala Mata is a goddess who helps people who are sick, especially those who are sick with small pox. It is said that Shitala Mata has the ability to purify blood, destroy germs, and reduce fever. She is called "the cooling one."

Small pox was a horrible disease that caused many people to die through the ages. Small pox caused high fever and a horrible rash that left scars. Small pox was stopped by use of immunizations. The last small pox case in the world was in 1977.

Shitala Mata is shown as a young maiden who is riding a donkey. She always wears a beautiful red dress and has a crown on her head. Sometimes she has two arms and sometimes she has four arms.

Shitala Mata carries a silver broom, a fan, a small bowl, and a pot of water. She uses these items to remove disease from houses. She sweeps up the germs with her broom. Then she uses the fan to collect them. She dumps them into the bowl and then the germs are banished. She then sprinkles water from the pot to purify the house. This is water that came from the river Ganges, which is in India. The Ganges is considered a sacred river.

Judaism

Donkeys are the most frequently mentioned animal in the Old Testament of the Bible, especially in the Torah, the first five books. The Torah presents the origin of Jewish people, the Israelites. These stories tell of their trials and challenges and their covenant with their Lord. Many of the stories in the Old Testament speak of donkeys. The donkeys are always providing service.

Moses led the Jews across the desert as they escaped from Egypt. This is called he Exodus. Their belongings were carried by donkeys. The Lord commanded the Israelites not to take horses with them when they escaped. Horses were considered a symbol of wealth, war, power, and the military. The Israelites did not use horses and chariots to fight battles. They valued donkeys for their helpful service. In an ancient Jewish synagogue, a beautiful mosaic of a pair of donkeys was recently found.

The Petter Chamor or Redemption of the Firstborn Donkey, is a mitzvah or commandment in Judaism. In this mitzvah, a male firstborn donkey is redeemed by the owner of the donkey. The owner gives a lamb or kid to the priest in exchange for the baby donkey. The goal of the mitzvah is to help people be reminded that their possessions, including animals, must be used for spiritual growth or else they lead to destruction. The mitzvah is performed in a synagogue, the Jewish place of worship.

Balaam's Donkey

The story of Balaam's donkey is in the Book of Numbers in the Old Testament. Balaam was hired by the enemies of the Israelites to set a curse on them. Balaam was traveling by donkey to where the Israelites were camped. This angered the Lord. The Lord sent his angel to stand in the path with a sword. Balaam did not see the angel, but his donkey did. His donkey pulled Balaam into a field to avoid the danger. Balaam hit his donkey because he was angry.

The angel presented danger to Balaam three times. Every time, the donkey saw the danger, but Balaam could not see the angel or the danger. Every time, the donkey protected Balaam by moving him out of the way from the danger. Every time, Balaam got angry and hit his donkey.

Finally, the Lord allowed the donkey to speak. The donkey said: "What have I done to you to make you beat me these three times? Am I not your own donkey, which you have always ridden, to this day? Have I been in the habit of doing this to you?" The Lord then opened Balaam's eyes and he saw the angel. The angel told Balaam that if his donkey had not protected him, he would have been killed. Balaam repented.

Note that what the donkey said appears to be a question based on the "Golden Rule." The Golden Rule focuses on treating others how we want them to treat us. There is a version of the Golden Rule in every religion and spiritual doctrine in the world. It appears that a very early statement of the Golden Rule was made by a donkey. Always remember what Balaam's donkey said when you are interacting with others.

CHRISTIANITY

Mary and Joseph

There are many beautiful works of art that show Mary riding a donkey as Joseph led them to Bethlehem, where Jesus was born. There is no scripture in the Bible that says that Mary rode a donkey.

The Bible does say that Mary and Joseph traveled from Nazareth to Bethlehem. This is a journey of 90 miles or 145 kilometers. It would take 4 to 6 days of walking to make this trip. Do you think a pregnant woman, who was about ready to give birth, could have walked this far? Likely not.

During this time, that donkeys were ridden in such travels. So it is almost certain that Mary rode a donkey to Bethlehem. It is also likely that the donkey stayed in the stable where Jesus was born.

After the birth of Jesus, Joseph received a warning from an angel telling him to flee to Egypt with Mary and Jesus. Paintings of this trip show Mary riding a donkey with Jesus.

Jesus Entering Jerusalem

The story of how Jesus entered Jerusalem appears in Matthew in the New Testament. As Jesus, his disciples, and Mary Magdaline approached Jerusalem, they stopped on Mount of Olives. Jesus sent two disciples ahead, telling them to find a female donkey with a colt and to bring it to him to ride.

The reason that Jesus did this was because of a prophecy in the book of Zechariah in the Old Testament. The prophecy said, "Say to Daughter Zion, 'See, your king comes to you, gentle and riding on a donkey, and on a colt, the foal of a donkey."

The disciples went into the village and did as Jesus had instructed. They brought the donkey and her colt to Jesus. They placed their cloaks on the donkey for Jesus to sit on. A very large crowd came. People spread cloaks or cut palm branches from the trees and spread them on the road for the donkey carrying Jesus to walk on.

To understand the importance of how Jesus entered Jerusalem, remember that the purpose of donkeys was to serve and help people. Warriors rode horses or used horses to drive chariots to engage in battle to conquer other people. Riding a donkey, instead of a horse, was an important way for Jesus to say that he was coming in peace and to be of service. Donkeys teach us that we can all come in peace and be of service to others.

Islam

The prophet Muhammad, of the Islamic religion had a relationship with two special donkeys.

Ya`fūr

Muhammad rode a donkey whose name was Ya`fūr in his travels in the Middle East. It is said that Ya`fūr had the ability to speak and that Ya`fūr told Muhammad that he was the last of sixty generations of donkeys which had been used by prophets for riding. This included the prophets Abraham, Moses, and Jesus. Ya`fūr told Muhammad that he was the last of his line of donkeys because Muhammad was the last of the prophets. According to Islamic rule, Muhammad's face is not to be shown. Below is Jesus in his travels, riding on a the ancestor of Muhammad 's donkey, Ya`fūr.

Buraq

The story of Buraq is quote important to Muslims. Muhammad was in his home city of Mecca. While he was meditating, the angel Gabriel appeared to him. Gabriel brought Buraq. Buraq was a large white donkey with wings.

Muhammad got onto Buraq's back. Then Buraq, Muhammad, and Gabriel, flew to a mosque in Jerusalem. At this mosque, Muhammad prayed. Then, Buraq carried him up through the seven levels of heavens. While in these levels of heaven, Muhammad spent time talking with the earlier prophets. Then, at the highest level of heaven, Muhammad met with God. God instructed Muhammad to tell his followers that they were to offer prayers to God five times a day. Muhammad then came down from the seven heavens and flew back to Mecca on Baraq. He told his followers what he had seen and been told.

Muslims pray five times a day. They pray at dawn, midday, afternoon, sunset, and evening. This prayer is called the Salat. Muslims face the holy city of Mecca when they pray.

Chinese Legend

Zhang Guo Lao is said to have lived during the Tang Dynasty, which is from the 7th to 10th centuries. Zhang was the eldest of eight "immortals" according to the Chinese legend. Immortal means does not die. It was said that Zhang was more than 3,000 years old. He lived secluded in Zhong Tiao Mountain in Shanxi Province.

Each time Zhang traveled, he rode his white donkey. He rode with his back to the road ahead of him. Zhang could travel very long distances. Each time Zhang stopped to rest, he would fold his white donkey like a piece of paper and put it into a box. Then, when he wanted to continue, he would put water on the paper and it would become a real donkey again.

Many emperors during the Tang Dynasty called on Zhang Guo Lao so they could learn tips on living a long life. Zhang is said to have had magical abilities. Each time the emperors tried to visit him, he pretended that he was dead. As soon as the emperors left, he returned to life.

Zhang's magic trick of appearing to die to avoid conflict is is said to have taught a lesson to the Chinese people. This lesson is that it is best to avoid conflict and controversy, if at all possible.

Donkey as a Spirit Animal

Shamanism is an ancient healing tradition and a way of life. Shamanism describes the ancient spiritual practices of indigenous cultures. It is a way to connect with nature and all of creation. It is the shamanic understanding that people have spirit animals. A spirit animal is considered a teacher or guide that comes in the form of an animal.

People have different spirit animals. They may have a spirit animal who stays with them for a long time and other spirit animals who step in to help during specific times. Every spirit animal is thought to bring a set of traits that are important to the person they are connected with. The donkey is a spirit animal. Donkeys symbolize intelligence, determination, dedication, and faith in the creative force.

Donkeys are known to be hard workers. Donkeys are willing to take on the responsibilities and burdens of others by offering service. Donkeys encourage us to be of service. Donkey have big ears that can pick up sound from a long way off. They know how to listen for messages within the sounds. Donkeys encourage us to pay close attention to what is happening around us and to trust our gut instincts. Donkeys evolved in rocky terrain. If they sense danger, they stop and then look closely. Donkeys encourage us to stop and think about what is happening before taking any further action and to look for a safe way to resolve the situation, rather than simply running away.

Donkeys can be perceived to be stubborn. They are being self-protective. They trust, respect, and listen to their own intuitive senses–their "gut feelings." They know their boundaries and what they can and can't do. Donkeys show us how to stick to doing what we know is best for us. Donkeys teach us determination. They are dedicated and work hard. But they still grow tired. The only reason they go on is because they are determined to do so. Donkeys encourage us to keep going when things get tough.

Following the Way of the Donkey

Following The Way of the Donkey

Donkey EEAW! ~ Donkey Enabled Empowerment and Wisdom

Donkeys have "traits" that social scientists tell us help people feel happy and empowered—and to respond effectively when things get tough. A trait is a quality or behavior that everyone in a group has.

Support Your Happiness and Empowerment

Some of the best ways to feel happy and empowered are these:

- **Connect With Friends.** Donkeys have special buddies and connect with many friends.
- **Reach Out To Be Kind.** Donkeys scratch each other's backs. They are kind and of service to others.
- **Build Your Strengths.** Donkeys like to learn new things.
- **Focus on the Good.** Donkeys are very thankful—especially if you bring carrots.

If you do these four things that donkeys do, this can help you feel happy and empowered.

If Things Get Tough…

Unfortunately, there may be times in your life when things get tough. Someone may be bullying you. You might have just broken up with a friend. You may have gotten into a fight with your sister or brother. Your family may have to move, which means you have to go to a new school and make new friends. Your parents could be having a fight or maybe they are getting a divorce. You may be having problems with your studies. A loved one could have just died.

Sometimes bad things just happen. This is not fair. But this is what it is.

Remember when we learned about how donkeys respond when they sense danger or they are not sure. They do this:

- **Stop and Stay Calm.** Donkeys stop and stay calm. They do not overreact.
- **Stand Tall.** Donkeys stand tall to appear and feel powerful.
- **Think Things Through.** Donkeys think things through to decide what is best to do.

If you follow the three things that donkeys do, this can help you if things get tough.

THE WAY OF YOUR BRAIN

To understand why following The Way of the Donkey can help you feel happy and empowered and respond effectively when things get tough, it is helpful to understand how your brain works.

Happiness and Empowerment

The working parts of your brain are the neurons. Neurons are cells in the brain and nervous system that communicate with other cells to send messages to your body. These messages guide what you normally think about and how you respond. Neurons form connections, called "synapses," with other neurons. We say that these neurons are "wired together." Neurons send messages to each other through these synapses. These messages guide what we normally think about and how we normally respond.

Unfortunately, our brains evolved to pay more attention to bad things than good things. The reason for this was survival. Primitive people had to worry about dangerous animals along their path. Because of the way our brain evolved, our neurons are more likely to "wire together" in a way that keeps our attention focused on bad experiences or how bad we feel–and not pay attention to the good things that are happening that can make us feel happy and empowered. The really good news is that you can rewire the neurons in your brain to focus more on the good things and less on the bad things.

When Things Get Tough

It is also important to learn how to not "flip your lid." You can envision your brain this way. Fold your thumb down into the palm of your hand. Then fold your fingers over this. We will focus on two parts:

- The Little Brain, where your thumb is.
- The Big Brain, where your fingers are.

The Little Brain part is the oldest part of the brain–the amygdala. This goes into action when we think we are in danger. Our neurons send hormones throughout our bodies to prepare us to go into flight or to fight. This is so we can get away or protect ourselves from that dangerous animal. These days, when things get tough our Little Brain still responds like we might be facing a dangerous animal.

The Big Brain, our prefrontal cortex, is where we think things through, so we can make good decisions. Humans have a well-developed prefrontal cortex. We can think things through better than animals can.

A problem is that when we think there might be danger, this may cause us to "flip our lids." Open your fingers. If your Big Brain is no longer able to communicate with your Little Brain, your have "flipped your lid." You cannot think things through to decide what is best to do.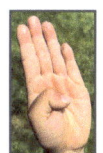

Amazingly, even though donkey's brains are not as sophisticated as human brains, donkeys have special traits that we can learn about and practice that can help us to not "flip our lid." Donkeys stop and remain calm, stand tall, and think things through. This can help you respond effectively when things get tough.

CONNECT WITH FRIENDS

I make positive connections with good friends and trusted adults.

Connect With Friends

I make positive connections with good friends and trusted adults.

Donkeys connect with their best "buddy donkey" in the pasture. It is said that "an only donkey is a lonely donkey." In any larger group of donkeys, there are smaller groups of two or three donkeys who are "best friends." Donkeys also make friends with other animals and their human friends.

Having good friends can help you feel good about yourself and have more fun in your life. To have good friends, you have to be a good friend. Pay attention to making positive connections with others. Smiling sends a message that you want to connect with others.

The biggest barrier to making friends is fear that someone might not want to be your friend. To deal with this fear, just focus on getting to know someone better. If you both decide to become friends, this is great. If not, that is also fine. Thinking this way can help you to relax and just have fun.

The best way to make new friends is by doing the things you enjoy. Is there a club or team you want to join or a class you want to take? Get involved in these activities with the idea of enjoying the activity–and possibly making a new friend. Focus on having fun doing what you like to do. Look around to find someone who also looks like they are having fun and start to talk to this person. People like to be friends with those who have fun doing the things they like to do.

Be the friend that you want to have. Treat people the way you want to be treated. Make sure that you are giving as much to your friend as you are receiving. Let your friends know that you believe in them and support them. Also, be sure to give your friends space. Everybody needs time by themselves.

Realize that friendships sometime end. This does not mean anything is wrong with either of you. Do not allow your sadness to turn to anger or attack. Keep yourself busy doing things that you enjoy. Be open to making new friends.

It is also helpful to have adult friends, especially some "trusted adults." Trusted adults are adults you feel safe talking to when you are upset or scared and really need some guidance on what you might do. It is helpful to have a number of trusted adults who you can talk to.

Trusted adults can be parents, grandparents, or guardians. A teacher or a coach could be a trusted adult. The parent of a friend could also be a trusted adult. Look around and you will find adults who would love to be friends with you.

Conduct a friendship audit. Who are your current friends? What interests do you share? What are the strengths of these friendships? How can you build on these strengths? How can you make new friends? What trusted adults do you connect with? How can you connect with other trusted adults?

At the end of the day, think to yourself: Who did you connect with today and how did this make you feel?

REACH OUT TO BE KIND

I reach out to be kind to others.

I act in service to others.

Reach Out To Be Kind

I reach out to be kind to others. I act in service to others.

Donkeys scratch each other's back. This is called "social grooming." Animals who live in social groups, like packs or herds, engage in social grooming. Social grooming helps animals bond in their group. Mother animals use social grooming to bond with their children. Social grooming is a way to resolve conflict–a way animals say, "I'm sorry."

As you can tell from the history of donkeys from early times, donkeys can teach us the importance of acting in a way that is in service to others.

One of the best ways you can increase your happiness is to consistently reach out to be kind to others. You might think that being kind to others is something you do for them. Being kind to others also is really good for you. Doing things in service to others also will make you feel really good about yourself.

Being kind to others makes you feel as good as the person you were kind to. Being kind to others can significantly increase your happiness and decrease your feelings of being alone. Being kind to others and acting in service results in other people being kind to you and makes our world a better place.

Here is a fun way that can help you focus on reaching out to be kind: Get five bright copper pennies. Start the day with those pennies in your left pocket. When you reach out to be kind to someone, transfer a penny over to your right pocket. Try to transfer all of those pennies to your right pocket. At the end of the day, think to yourself:

- Who did I reach out to be kind to?
- What did I do to be kind?
- How did this person respond?
- How did this make me feel?

Are there some other students in your school who you are not close to? Reach out to be kind to them. Is there someone in your school who is being excluded or treated badly? Reach out to be kind to this person. Has someone been hurtful to you in the past? Reach out to be kind to this person. Is there someone you would like to become friends with? Reach out to be kind to this person.

If someone has been hurtful to you, one way to respond is to create a "Ripple of Kindness." As quickly as you can, reach out to be kind to five people. Tell them you are starting a "Ripple of Kindness" and ask each of them to help you spread this Ripple by reaching out to be kind to five other people. Watch the Ripple grow. By shifting your focus from what happened to you to reaching out to be kind to others, this can help to take the pain of what happened away. This is a way to keep your positive personal power.

You could also help to form a Kindness Team at your school. This can be a great way to be of service to others. Conduct an online search for "kindness, school" for cool ideas.

Build Your Strengths

I use my personal strengths every day.

I build new strengths.

If things get tough, I use my strengths.

Build Your Strengths

I use my personal strengths every day. If things get tough, I use my strengths. I build new strengths.

Donkeys are very smart and like to learn new things. When you use your personal strengths to do new things, this makes you feel more empowered. Below are the character strengths that scientists from throughout the world think are the most important. Everybody has different strengths.

As you read this list, ask yourself: Is this a lot like me? Somewhat like me? Not much like me at this time?

- **Creativity**. I like to think of new and better ways of doing things.
- **Curiosity**. I am always asking questions and love to discover new things.
- **Judgement**. I look at all sides of an issue to come up with the right answer.
- **Love of Learning**. I love to learn new things.
- **Wisdom**. I am considered wise, because I think things through.
- **Bravery**. I speak up for what is right, even when others do not agree with me.
- **Persevere**. I finish what I start, even if it becomes difficult.
- **Honesty**. I speak the truth and I take responsibility for my feelings and behaviors.
- **Zest**. I live life as an adventure filled with excitement.
- **Love**. I value the close relationships I have with others.
- **Kindness**. I enjoy helping others, even if I do not know them well.
- **Social Intelligence.** I pay attention to how others are thinking and feeling.
- **Teamwork**. I always do my part and I work hard for the success of my group.
- **Fairness**. I treat all people fairly.
- **Leadership**. I am good at leading others.
- **Forgiveness**. I am willing to forgive someone who has done something wrong.
- **Humility**. I am humble and let my actions speak more than my words.
- **Prudence**. I am careful about what I do and try not to do things I might later regret.
- **Self-Control.** I am in control of what I do and say.
- **Appreciate Excellence**. I appreciate the beautiful and wonderful things in life.
- **Gratitude**. I pay attention to the good things that happen to me and say thanks.
- **Hope**. I believe that good things are coming to me now.
- **Humor**. I like to laugh, smile, and see the fun in all situations.
- **Spirituality**. I feel my life has a higher purpose.

Ask yourself: What are my best strengths? What strengths would I like to build?

At the beginning of each day, pick a strength you want to use or build. That day, do something that uses this strength. At the end of the day, think about how you used this and other strengths. If there is a problem you have to deal with, think things through to decide what to do that uses your strengths.

Focus on the Good

I focus on the good things that are happening in my life.

I am thankful and express my gratitude.

Focus on the Good

I focus on the good things that are happening in my life. I am thankful and express my gratitude.

Donkeys are very thankful when they receive treats–especially carrots or apples. They are also very thankful when they are being petted or groomed and when they can find a log to rub against. Most of all, they are thankful when they have loving people who take care of them.

Being thankful for good things makes you feel happy. Remember those neurons. When you intentionally focus on the good things that are happening in your life, this will wire your brain to be happier. If life has been challenging for you, intentionally reminding yourself every day to focus on the good and be thankful is one of the best ways to rewire your brain to regain happiness.

Here is a process you can use to be thankful for the good things that will help to wire or rewire your brain to be happy:

- **Have a Good Experience**. Either notice that a good thing that has happened or do something good for yourself.
- **Enrich It.** Keep thinking about this experience for just a bit of time. Even just a minute. Enjoy it. Think about how wonderful this is. Take the time to feel really happy.
- **Absorb It.** Think about this good experience as being absorbed into you. Let this happy feeling travel deep into your mind and warm your heart.

If you have a negative thought or something challenging has happened, think to yourself "cancel." Then, focus on a positive experience you recently had–one of those happy times you absorbed into your mind and heart. Let the good thoughts of this positive experience erase the negative.

At the end of each day, think about what happened that was good and that you are thankful for. You could even write about this in a "gratitude" journal. Gratitude is being thankful. Then, if you have a bad thought, think "cancel" and read through your gratitude journal.

If someone has done something that has made you feel happy, express your gratitude. Send a message to this person thanking them. This will make both you and them feel happy.

Try this experiment: Think about how happy you feel right now on a scale from 1 to 10–from "not happy much of the time" up to "very happy all of the time." Then, keep a gratitude journal for 30 days. At the end of each day write about three or more things that happened that made you feel happy. Spend a bit more time enriching and absorbing these happy feelings. Send a message or send positive thoughts to at least one person who did something that made you happy. Then, at the end of 30 days, think about how happy you feel on that 1 to 10 scale.

STOP AND STAY CALM

I sit quietly and achieve calm.

If things get tough, I remind myself to remain calm.

STOP AND STAY CALM

I sit quietly, am mindful, and achieve calm. If things get tough, I remind myself to remain calm.

Remember what donkeys do if they sense possible danger. They do not "flip their lids." They do not run away. They stop and stay calm. This is the best thing you can do if things get tough.

Practice Mindfulness

The practice of mindfulness helps people achieve calmness and focus and to "self-regulate." Self-regulate means that you have the ability to keep yourself calm. When you practice being mindful this will rewire your brain so that you are less likely to "flip your lid" if things get tough. Spend some time each day practicing mindfulness. There are some simple steps you can take to practice mindfulness.

- Take a seat on the floor and cross your legs or sit in a chair and make sure your feet are flat on the floor.
- Straighten your upper body but do not be stiff. Put your hands onto the tops of your legs.
- Drop your chin a little and either look down or close your eyes.
- Breathe in slowly. Hold your breath briefly. Slowly let your breath out.
- If your mind wanders, just return to thinking about your breath.
- Do this for at least a minute and work up to being able to do this for 5 minutes.

Remain Calm

If things get tough, it is important to remain calm. There are stages of "flipping your lid:"

- **Calm.** You feel calm and relaxed.
- **Trigger**. Something happens that starts making you feel upset.
- **Upset**. You become increasingly upset. You start to "flip your lid."
- **Outburst**. You become out of control. You have "flipped your lid" and cannot think clearly.
- **Confusion**. You now feel confused and embarrassed.
- **Recovery**. The time it takes for you to calm down.

Trust your gut instincts. When you have triggered or are about to trigger, pay close attention to remaining calm. Use your mindfulness skills. Breathe in slowly, hold your breath briefly, slowly let your breath out. Walk away from the situation, if you can. Practice mindfulness until you have calmed.

At a time when you are calm, think about what makes you trigger. Think about how and where this might occur. Then think about your strengths and how you can use each of your strengths if something starts to trigger you? If something happens and you start to trigger, remain calm by breathing slowly. Use one of your strengths to effectively respond.

Stand Tall

I stand tall and walk with pride.

I do not allow what happens to control how I think about myself or respond.

Stand Tall

I stand tall and walk with pride. I do not allow what happens to control how I think about myself or respond.

Donkeys are "animals of prey." Animals of prey means that other animals might eat them. A donkey who is feeling threatened or is not sure what might be happening will stand very tall to appear powerful.

Stand With Power

Standing tall indicates higher power, whereas hunching over and keeping your arms crossed over your chest reflects lower power. Standing tall communicates "I have the power to effectively handle this." Try this for yourself:

- **First, "feel small."** Stand or sit in a hunched over manner. Hang your head low. Look down at your feet. Fold your arms across your chest. Take a breath and sigh. How does this make you feel?
- **Now, "stand tall."** Stand up as straight as you can. Hold your head high. Look directly in front of you. Hold your arms high in a "success pose"–like you would hold your hands if you just scored a soccer goal or got an "A" on a paper. Say, "Yeah! Right on!" How does this make you feel?

When you stand tall, this makes you feel more powerful–even when inside you might be feeling small. Stand tall whenever you feel you need more personal power. Every morning, before you leave your house, take a minute to practice standing tall and feeling empowered. If something happens that might cause you to "flip your lid," first breathe slowly to remain calm and then remind yourself to stand tall.

Control Your Thinking

You will never be able to control when or if someone is hurtful to you or something bad happens. You do have the ability to control your thinking about how you feel about yourself and will respond.

Feeling sad or angry is not just caused by the bad things that happen to us but also by our beliefs about those things. We can't control what might happen. We can control our beliefs. Think about this as A-B-C:

- **A is the "adversity."** Adversity is the bad thing that has happened.
- **C is the "consequence."** The consequence is how you feel or the outcome.

But A is <u>not the only thing</u> that causes C.

- **B is your "belief."** Your belief is what you think or believe about A, not merely that A happened.

Thus, A + B = C. While it is not possible to control A, it is possible to control B, and in this way be in control of C. When you know you can control C you will feel more empowered.

In other words think to yourself: I don't always have control over what happens to me but I can control how I feel about myself and respond and in this way, I can control the outcome. I can stand tall despite what happens. I can be positively powerful!

Think Things Through

When things get tough, I think things through to decide what to do.

Think Things Through

When things get tough, I think things through to decide what to do.

Donkeys are sometimes considered to be stubborn. What they are doing is protecting themselves. Before they do something, they will think things through to decide if this is the best thing for them to do. Donkeys want to be in control of what they will do.

When you learn how to effectively think things through, you are better able to take care of yourself and come up with a good approach to respond if things get tough.

Think Things Through

This is how you can think things through to decide what is best to do:

- **What has happened?** Take the time to think about what has happened to make sure you have an accurate understanding.
- **What is my goal?** Know what you want to achieve. If you made a mistake and were hurtful or acted inappropriately, be sure to accept responsibility and take steps to make things right.
- **What strategies could I use?** Identify several different strategies that you could use. Identify strategies that use your strengths..
- **Is each strategy in accord with my values?** Evaluate the strategies based on your own values.
- **For each, what might happen?** Think about what might happen if you followed each strategy.
- **What is my best choice?** Decide which strategy would be your best first choice.
- **How should I proceed?** Determine what steps are necessary to implement this strategy.
- **Did this work?** Evaluate the effectiveness. Realize that the first thing you try might not work.
- **If not, what else could I do?** Repeat this process if the first strategy you tried did not work.

Create Goals and Plan Your Actions

Another way you can think things through is by creating goals and an action plan. Create goals that you want to achieve, because this is important to you. Make sure your goals are specific and something you can do. Put your goals in writing.

Then plan your actions. Think things through to identify the steps necessary. Decide what needs to happen first and then next. Identify when each step has been taken. Evaluate the effectiveness of your actions. Revise your plan as necessary.

Take time at the start of each day or week to identify a goal for what you want to do and create an action plan. At the end of the day or week, think about how you did. Then create a new goal or revise your action plan.

Photo Credits

PD means Public Domain either because the copyright has expired, image of the U.S. Federal Government, or the image has been placed into the Public Domain. Wikimedia means that the image has been placed into the Wikimedia Creative Commons for public use. Pixabay means the image was found on the Pixabay free images site. UP means Used with Permission.

The donkey on the Chapter pages was drawn by Robin Nilsson.

Donkey Faces: Jennifer Wasson, UP. Becky Teal, U.P. Debra Means, UP. Laurie Richardson, UP. Peggy Curtis, Crown Meadow Miniature Donkeys, http://crownmeadow.com/, UP. Heather Andreini, UP. Becky Miller, UP. AnnaER, Pixabay. Editonevideo, Pixabay. Equine Rescue Network at https://www.facebook.com/EquineRescueNetwork/, UP. Amber Meier, UP. Heather Andreini, UP.

Let's Learn About Donkeys

Page 2. Donkey ear, Jaclou-DL, Pixabay. Laughing donkey, Kat Butler, UP. Author.

Page 3. Girl, Kelly Arey, UP. Boy, Author. Man and daughter, Noah Lemke & Tayler Brentano, Heirloom Ranch, https://www.facebook.com/heirloomranchoregon/, UP.

Page 4. Donkey colors, author's donkeys and Páramo woolly baby donkey, Patricio Mena Vásconez, Wilimedia. Poitou donkey, Sudorculus, Wikimedia. Sleek donkey, JamesDemers, Pixabay. Boy grooming, Joni Straker, UP. Girl grooming, Steve Stiert, Donkey Park, http://donkeypark.org, Barbara J. Raskopf Shapiro, photographer, UP. Farrier, Gabriel Shenberg, UP.

Page 5. Eohippus By Heinrich Harder (1858-1935) - The Wonderful Paleo Art of Heinrich Harder, PD.

Chestnut horse in field. Karen Arnold, Wikimedia. Zebra at wildlife reserve Paul Brennan, Wikimedia. Donkey, cocolecourt, Pixabay.

Page 6. Wild African Ass baby, T.Voekler, Wikimedia. Somali wild ass (Equus africanus somaliensis) at the San Diego Zoo Wild Animal Park, California, Ericj, Wikimedia. Somali Wild Ass, Zoo Basel, Wikimedia.

Page 7. Kiger and Riddle Mountain Herd Management Areas, BLM, PD. wild donkey, Pack Burro and Racer, Jay Holland, Western Pack Burro ASS-ociation Photographer, http://www.packburroracing.com/, UP.

Page 8. Mule By Sogospelman at English Wikipedia, Wikimedia. Zonkey, TANGdesign, Dorte Tang, Wikimedia. Page 9. Baby donkeys. Peggy Curtis, Crown Meadow Miniature Donkeys, http://crownmeadow.com/, UP. Lori Wargo, Northend Acres Miniature Donkeys, http://www.northendacres.com, UP. New Miniature Donkey Foal, Kelly Fletcher, Wikimedia. Manfred Antranias Zimmer, Pixabay. Bru-nO, Pixabay. Lynn Fozzy, UP. Shelly Flora, PU. Miranda Brooke , UP. Tanjafroehlich, Pixabay. Ranrouha, Pixabay.

Page 10 Baby donkeys and kids. Girl in blue, Ray and Heather Zinn, Amazing Acres, http://amazinnacres.blogspot.com/, UP. Boy with 2 donkeys, Lori Wargo, Northend Acres Miniature Donkeys, http://www.northendacres.com, UP. Boy carrying donkey, Ruth Vanderlaan Vanderlaand the Barn Yard Zoo, http://thebarnyardzoo.com/. Boy in blue, Shelly Flora, UP. Teen in red, Holly Besaw, Kickin Up Dust, http://www.therapetsinc.org, UP. Girl in pink. Kelly Arey, UP. With mommoth baby, Noah Lemke & Tayler Brentano, Heirloom Ranch, https://www.facebook.com/heirloomranchoregon/, UP. Girl feeding, Miranda Brooks, UP. Girl in black, Maxine Girdlestone-Hayden. Dinky Donkey Adventures, https://www.facebook.com/pages/Dinky-Donkey-Adventures/, UP

Donkeys Through Time

Page 12. Fresco on the Tomb of Iti showing the transportation of wheat by donkey, PD. Donkey in an Egyptian painting c. 1298–1235 BC, PD. Burros en un relieve egipcio en piedra caliza, Imperio Antiguo, Museo Egipcio de Berlín.jpg, Carlos Teixdor Cadnas, Wikimedia. Donkeys in pyramid, Rossel, S., Marshall, F., Peters, J., Pilgram, T., Adams, M.D., and O'Connor, D. (March 11, 2008 105) Domestication of the donkey: Timing, processes, and indicators. Proceedings of the National Academy of Sciences. UP.

Page 13. Donkey with packs, circa 1991 –1450 B.C. , Metropolitan Museum of Art, Wikimedia. Two donkey carrying packs (1990-1786 BCE), Museum of Fine Arts Lyon, Rama, Wikimedia. Youth wearing a cucullus and leading his donkey, 1st century BC, Terracotta figurine from Taranto, Apulia, Magna Graecia, Wikimedia. Two boys with donkey Ancient Egyptian tomb figurines depicting workers loading up a couple of donkeys with supplies,2000 BC., Keith Schengili-Roberts, Wikimedia.

Page 14. Drunken Silenus, Roman mosaic, Naples National Archeological Museum, Jebulon. Wikimedia. Donkey Fed by a Youth, Imperial Palace Mosaic Museum, PD. Roman mosaic donkey and grapes, Byzantinischer Mosaizist des 5. Jahrhunderts - The Yorck Project, PD.

Page 15. Silk road map, Jyusin, Wikimedia. Caravane sur la Route de la soie, PD. Chinese man on donkey, PD.

Page 16. Landing of Columbus (12 October 1492), painting by John Vanderlyn, PD. The Pirámide del Sol at Teotihuacan, Daniel Case, Wikimedia . The Aztecs Pyramid at St. Cecilia Acatitlan, Mexico State, Maunus, Wikimedia. The MaWikimediahu PiWikimediahu, in Peru, at twilight, Martin St-Amant. Wikimedia.

Page 17. Advertisement for Royal Gift, Mt Vernon, PD. Woman's Land Army, Calif. [between ca. 1915 and ca. 1920], Library of Congress, PD. Plowing with a mule, sowing sericea lespedeza by hand in Sumner County, Tennessee, Tennessee State Library and Archives, Nashville, TN, Wikimedia.

Page 18. Wilhelm Hester Photographs Collection, PD. Nome Gold Rush, Nichols, C. D., Library of Congress, PD. The Prospector, unknown, PD. "Wanderers of the Wastelands" vintage postcard of an unknown prospector and his burros, Orange County Archives, PD.

Page 19. Tanya Hancock, A Donkeys Trust (public group on Facebook), UP.

Page 20. Historical Geography, 1900, Italy, Sicily, Toy beast of burden from Sardinia, PD.. Aboard the Sicilian festival cart are the Italian Royal children, approx 1911, PD. Particolare di un carretto siciliano. Pittura ad opera del maestro Damiano Rotella, Carrettosiciliano Miniature donkey, Wikimedia. Little Rasscal's Crimson Clover, 2018 National Champion Miniature Donkey, Owned, shown and trained by Shannon Barlow, Texas Lonestar LongEars, https://www.facebook.com/Texas-Lonestar-Longears-TXLL.

Page 21. Lt. Richard Alexander "Dick" Henderson using a donkey to carry a wounded soldier at the Battle of Gallipoli, PD. Two German soldiers and their mule wearing gas masks in World War One, 1916, PD. Pte John Simpson Kirkpatrick stands next to his donkey, PD. American Donkey Corps in World War II, Italian theater in World War II, PD.

Page 22. The Baby's own Aesop: being the fables condensed in rhyme with portable morals pictorially pointed by Walter Crane; 1908; F. Warne, New York. PD.

Page 23. Illustration of a Grimm fairy tale, "The Travelling Musicians" By Baudry, PD. Illustration of a Grimm fairy tale, "The Travelling Musicians" or "The Bremen Town-Musicians", 1876, George Cruikshank

Page 24. PD photographs from Wikimedia Commons.

Donkeys Now

Page 26. Donkey in desert, jacqueline macou, Pixabay. African children in donkey cart, Lynn Greyling, Pixabay. Hard work by a donkey in Georgia, PMATAS, Wikimedia. Donkey as a working animal in MoroWikimediao Africa By Ab5602 , Wikimedia.. ågne saetchant ene Wikt:drôvate, Lucyin, Wikimedia. ågne avou on bassa, Lucyin, Wikimedia. African women always working in Ziniare, Burkina Faso, Jeff Attaway, Wikimedia. ågne tcheriant ås djåbes, Lucyin, Wikimedia. Donkey pulling cart during the Carnival of Huejotzingo, Puebla, Mexico, Thelmadatter, Wikimedia. Donkeys in San Miguel De Allende, Lisa DiAntonio, Pixabay. Ezel in de Colca vallei man with donkey in peru, Smiley.toerist , Wikimedia. Woman riding on a donkey in the mountains in Tunisia, Peter van der Sluijs, Wikimedia. Iraqi girls on a donkey cart through the streets of Abu Atham, Iraq, James (Jim) Gordon, Wikimedia.

Page 27-30. Look into eyes, Sue Snyder, UP. Kissing, Julie Fluckey, UP. Girl with spotted, Laurie Richardson, UP. Boy in red, Clair, Creed, UP. Reading book, Kat Butler, UP. Hoodie look, Shannon Costello, UP. Girl in pink, Wendy Wilson, UP. Hold face, Steve Stiert, Donkey Park, http://donkeypark.org, Barbara J. Raskopf Shapiro, photographer, UP. Red bucket, Nathan School, UP. Hold hands, Happy Donkey Tours, https://www.happydonkeytours.com/, UP. Barrels, Traci Ross, UP. Riding with ball, Amanda Brookel, UP. Boy on mammoth, Kris wilcox, UP. Obstacles, Becca Babolian, UP. Leading mammoth, Sue Snyder, TP. Climbing on, Nicole Mauro, UP. Grooming, Hyacinth Fiorenzo, UP. Obstacles, Becca Babolain, UP. Girl in red, Lorna Da Sha, UP. Amazed at donkey, author. Purple coat, Shannan Usiak, UP. Girl in hat with mammoth, Nathalie Lepang, UP. Boy in blue, yellow hat, and other boy in blue, Steve Stiert, Donkey Park, http://donkeypark.org, Barbara J. Raskopf Shapiro, photographer, UP. Girl in plaid dress, author. Boy with apple, Lacy Gray, UP. Girl hugging, Christine Hearst, UP. Fall harvasst, Ann Firestone, UP. Mermaid, Carey Hoff, UP. Winter hat, Kelly Arey, UP. Girl in red, Deborah Clark, UP. Halloween pants, Denise White, UP. Halloween photo, Lacy Gray, UP. Christmas photo, Heidi Sloan, UP.

Page 31. Donkey show. Girl leading, Carey Hoff, UP. Girl in costume, Ray and Heather Zinn, Amazing Acres, http://amazinnacres.blogspot.com/, UP. Woman in mountain trail, Meredith Bakula, UP. Boy leading, Shannon Barlow and Natalie Woods, Texas Lonestar LongEars, http://www.longearstx.com, UP. Boy riding mountain trail, author. Cart, Meredith Bakula, UP. Barrels, Kelly Dehnel, Olympic Miniature Donkeys, UP. Jumping, Meredith Hodges of Lucky Three Ranch on Little Jack Horner, https://www.luckythreeranch.com/UP. Winning girl, Meredith Bakula, UP.

Page 32. Wild Burros in the wild, in a pen, with girl, BLM, PD. Donkey being ridden and packed, Kimberly Biafora, UP. Freeze brand, author.

Page 33. Pack Burro Racing, Photos by Western Pack Burro ASS-ociation Photographers, Jennifer Mewes, Jay Holland, Alison Conrad, Brian Miller, UP. http://www.packburroracing.com/

Page 34. Mountain Ridge Gear, https://www.mountainridgegear.com/ UP. Kimberly Biafora, UP. Amber Wann, UP.

Page 35. Happy Donkey Tours, https://www.happydonkeytours.com/, UP.

Page 36. Mule plowing, Festival of La Trilla of Castrillo de Villavega, Valdavia, Wikimedia. Meredith Hodges of Lucky Three Ranch on Lucky Three Sundowner, https://www.luckythreeranch.com/UP. Mule Pack String on Lion Fire, US Forest Service, PD. Guide leading mule riders up a steep portion of the Bright Angel Trail known as Heartbreak Hill, NPS, Michael Quinn, PD.

Page 37. Maxine Girdlestone-Hayden. Dinky Donkey Adventures, https://www.facebook.com/pages/Dinky-Donkey-Adventures/, UP. Amber Wann, Rocky Mountain Beverage Burro, https://www.facebook.com/RockyMountainBeverageBurro/, UP. Becky Miller, UP.

Page 38. Amber Wann, Rocky Mountain Beverage Burro, https://www.facebook.com/RockyMountainBeverageBurro/, UP. Amber Photos, Julian and Tracy Austwick (2016) *Amber's Donkey: The Heart-Warming Tale of How a Donkey and a Little Girl Healed the Scars of Each Other's Troubled Pasts*, https://www.facebook.com/Ambersdonkey/, UP. Holly Besaw, Kickin Up Dust, http://www.therapetsinc.org, UP. Harrison photos, Hal Walter, (2016) *Full Tilt Boogie: A journey into autism, fatherhood, and an epic test of man and beast*, https://hardscrabbletimes.com/, UP.

Page 39. Injury photos, PD. Daisy photos, Jen Morton, UP. Piper photos, Sara Evancho, ttps://www.facebook.com/PiperTheTherapyDonkey/, UP. Hazel the Donkey & Christopher Ameruoso, Christopher Ameruoso Hazel is a rescue donkey at Spirit of Animals ranch, UP.

Page 40. Donkey basketball photos from news articles. Use is based on Fair Use for Comment and Criticism.

Spiritual Donkeys

Page 42. Dionysus on a Donkey, dated 2nd century, PD. Dionysus and Hephaestus riding ass, Athenian black-figure kylix C6th B.C., Museum of Fine Arts Boston, PD. Hephaestus on Donkey. Athenian red-figure drinking cup, 5th century, Toledo Museum of Art, PD.

Page 43. An artistic depiction of Hindu goddess Shitala, Jonoikobangali, Wikimedia. 3rd quarter of 19th century By Unknown, PD.

Page 44. Panels of a mosaic floor in a Late Roman (fifth-century) synagogue at Huqoq, an ancient Jewish village, Baylor University, PD. Donkey at Petter Chamor, Lori Wargo, Northend Acres Miniature Donkeys, http://www.northendacres.com, UP.

Page 45. Balaam and the Angel, 1836, Gustav Jäger, PD.

Page 46. Joseph and Mary arrive in Bethlehem, The life of Jesus of Nazareth, 1906, William Hole, PD. Flight to Egypt, 1304-6, Giotto di Bondone, The Yorck Project (2002), PD.

Page 47. Jesus entering Jerusalem on a donkey, early 1900s, unknown, unknown publisher of Bible Card, PD. -Jesus entering Jerusalem, 1873, The story of the Bible from Genesis to Revelation, unknown, PD.

Page 48. Entry into Jerusalem, Life of Christ, 1300's, Giotto di Bondone, Scrovegni Chapel, PD. Reproduction of 17th century Indian (Mughal) miniature, unknown, PD.

Page 49. A woodcut of Zhang Guo, carrying a fish-drum, unknown, PD. Chinese painting, unknown, PD.

Page 50. Julie Fluckey, UP.

The Way of the Donkey

Page 53. Tashi and Keizen's hands. .

Page 54 Kathy 2408 Pixabay

Page 56. Ann Heffernan, UP

Page 58. 12019, Pixabay.

Page 60, Donkey with carrot, Clay Junell, Wikimedia.

Page 62. Wild burros, BLM, PD.

Page 64. A donkey in Dana Biosphere Reserve, Jordan, Bernard Gagnon, Wikimedia.

Page 66. 12019, Pixabay.

Page 67. Linda Drain, UP.